cezanne

cezanne

Text by
PAMELA PRITZKER

LEON AMIEL • PUBLISHER
NEW YORK

Published by
LEON AMIEL • PUBLISHER
NEW YORK
ISBN 0-8148-0661-9
Printed in the United States of America

The history of art is abundantly rich in tales of struggling artists, unrecognized in their genius until after their deaths. However, few of these artists persevered in their public and private struggles as did Paul Cezanne. Throughout his life, Cezanne fought against artistic prejudice, public ridicule, emotional instability and increasingly ill health. It was only towards the end of his life, that Cezanne glimpsed a small hope of critical success. It was only after his death, that hindsight proved to all the world the enormity of his genius by proclaiming Paul Cezanne the "Father of Modern Art".

Paul Cezanne was born on January 19, 1839 in Aix a small city in Provence. His father was a banker and exceedingly watchful over the family accounts. Cezanne's sister Marie and his mother were both devoted to him and encouraged young Cezanne to paint. His mother spoke to him often of the great Dutch Masters, Rembrandt and Rubens, and supplied him with his first box of paints. From that point onwards, Cezanne knew he must become a painter.

As a child, Cezanne had very few social contacts. Perhaps his parents' belated marriage, five years after his birth, set him apart from the more 'respectable' citizenry of provincial Aix. His father was driven to make and save money, at any cost. He was a miserly, strict authoritarian and a constant tease. Emile Zola, Cezanne's oldest friend, portrayed the very rigid structure of the Cezanne household in his novel, *The Conquest*.

Fortunately, at the age of thirteen, Cezanne was sent to the College Bourbon, releasing him from the tyranny of his father. It was at school that Cezanne became fast friends with Zola. Ironically, it was Zola who excelled in art classes, winning many of the school's prizes. Zola was not a native of Provence, causing him to be ostracized by his fellow classmates. Cezanne felt a kindred spirit in Zola and ignored the taunts of the other students. Together with a third friend, Baille they formed a modern day Three Musketeers. During the summer holidays, they spent long afternoons hunting, fishing and swimming in the Provencal countryside. It was during these idyllic summer days that Zola succeeded in freeing Cezanne's long repressed spirit. Frequently, the three budding young artists would bring sketch pads and spend hours devouring nature and the out-door life. Zola later captured this entire period in, *L'Oevre* and *The Confession*. Cezanne sought to embrace it in all of his paintings.

In 1856, the boys left the College as boarding

students. Upon returning to his home, Cezanne's dislike of his father intensified. His contempt for saving money was such that when Zola asked why he spent every last penny, Cezanne replied, "Par dieu, if I were to die tonight, would you want my parents to inherit?" At this point, Cezanne's father realized he would never join him at the bank, and began to encourage him to practice law.

By 1858, Cezanne was attending night classes at the free Drawing School in Aix, while finishing college during the day. Zola and his family were forced by financial reasons to move to Paris. This departure marked the beginning of a great prose-poetry correspondence between Emile Zola and Cezanne. Over the next several months, the two wrote of their unrequited loves, difficulties at college, praises of Hugo and Cicero and of all the new literature and life they began to experience. That summer, once again the three were reunited and spent two glorious months in the countryside. By the winter of 1858, all three had passed their exams and Zola returned to Paris. Cezanne remained in Aix to begin his studies in law.

From letters written to Zola, we know that Cezanne was greatly tormented during his stay in Aix. He felt a deep sense of desolation at being alone in Aix and worried greatly over money. It was a period of extreme anxiety, complicated by an inability to form relationships with women other than his mother and sister. In long, prosaic letters to Zola, Cezanne would extoll the beauty of some young girls he had momentarily fallen in love with, yet he could not make direct contact with the girl. In fact, he was afraid to reach out and touch a woman.

In addition to these problems, the relationship with his father disintegrated further. The entire family had moved to a large, Louis XIV mansion, surrounded by beautiful gardens and a bathing pool. Although his father provided him with a studio in the house, he could not justify Cezanne earning his living as a painter. The tensions between the two increased, but Cezanne was terrified of moving away from Aix. All the letters from Zola emphasized his impoverished condition in Paris. Zola was isolated, without true friends and without a job. However, Cezanne's father offered him a monthly allowance which would alleviate monetary problems and enable Cezanne to move to Paris. That following summer, Zola begged Cezanne to move to Paris. Yet, Cezanne felt compelled to complete his law studies before he could freely pursue his art. The rest of the year was spent by Cezanne studying art at night and law by day. In his painting Cezanne struggled to overcome his acute idealism and realize a precise and naturalistic image.

In April, 1861, Cezanne surmounted his fears

and left Aix. He arrived in Paris with a monthly allowance of 300 francs. Zola set up a daily work schedule for Cezanne. His mornings were spent at the Atelier Suisse, drawing and painting from live models. In the afternoon, he would spend hours with the great masters at the Louvre. Initially, he and Zola were inseperable, but gradually Cezanne withdrew into himself as he was accustomed to doing in Aix. He was in a state of confusion caused by the multiplicity of events confronting him. Furthermore, he could not as yet distinguish the works of the great masters from the academics, let alone evolve his own style. He began a portrait of Zola but their friendship remained strained due to Cezanne's erratic moods. Throughout that summer Cezanne fought to crystallize his ideas while assimilating new ones. In September, Cezanne returned to Aix, defeated and frustrated in his search for artistic revelation.

Upon his return, Cezanne repentently joined his father's bank. Several months passed and soon Cezanne was inexorably bored with the world of finance. His longing to be an artist intensified. Zola returned to Aix that summer and Cezanne began landscape painting. By the autumn, Cezanne's confidence was renewed and he returned to Paris.

This time the Louvre became a place of wonder

to Cezanne. He had discovered in the vibrant works of Delacroix the world of color. At the Atelier Suisse, Cezanne became acquainted with the young and rebellious artists who did not accept the Academy's definition of Art. It was through these friends that Cezanne met the second major influence in his life, Camille Pissarro.

Almost ten years his senior, Pissarro exerted a discipline over Cezanne which would affect all of his later works. Pissarro was an outsider, from the Virgin Islands, who like Cezanne, rejected a career in business for painting. He brought to France his practice of painting out-of-doors, as Cezanne had done in Aix. It was Pissarro who formulated much of the impetus for Impressionism. Through his painting out-of-doors, Pissarro realized the effects of natural lighting on objects and the inseperable relationship between the artist and nature. He chose to paint the objects realistically, as they were formulated by the effect of light. Manet, had taken this concept of natural light and jolted the art world with "Dejeuner sur l'herbe". By rejecting the traditional technique of chiaroscuro, Manet realistically rendered objects in the open-air. Although the critics were rocked with laughter, Cezanne was shakened to his very core. Pissarro and Manet had liberated one more constraint in his own technique. Cezanne fully embraced open-air painting along with a group of artists, who also felt the need for freedom, including Fantin-Latour, Monet, Degas, Pissarro, Bazille and Renoir. Together, this rebellious group explored the effects of light, and opened the doors to Impressionism.

Cezanne's own work during this explosive period was very awkward. His draftsmanship was not good and he had great difficulty in expressing the seething emotions within himself. The themes he chose were extremely violent dealing with rapes, murders, orgies and temptations. His style, although still very rough, was filled with dichotomies. He used thick, black outlines filled with vivid color to achieve a sense of solid mass. Oftentimes, he would apply the color in short, choppy brushstrokes, making the masses move from within. His own inner turmoil is represented by the ferocity of these early works.

In 1866, Cezanne was fully entrenched with the 'rebellious' painters, meeting with the informal group of future Impressionists most evenings at the Cafe Guerbois. At times, he would vociferously participate in the arguments concerning aesthetics and politics. However, at times when Manet was present, he would usually sit in a corner and scornfully eye the participants.

Cezanne continued to paint and submit his works to the Salon. Although he outwardly scorned the official exhibit, deriding it as the "Salon des Bozards", inwardly he yearned for the official acceptance by the Academy. This acceptance would bring substantial monetary rewards and approval from his father. Cezanne submitted two works, "An Afternoon at Naples, or the "Wine Grog" and "Woman with Flea", both of which were rejected. However, rather than depressing Cezanne, the rejection pleased him by placing him amongst the other 'true' artists who also were rejected. It was at this same time that his ferocious emotions as seen in "L'orgie", seem to harmonize with his technique of painting, as seen in "Uncle Dominic". The patient efforts of Pissarro apparently began to take form in Cezanne's works.

During the next two years, Cezanne developed an artistic personna. He dressed as a bohemian, spoke out for radical politics and stood against all bourgeois sentimentality. He joined with Monet, Zola, Pissarro and the other artists and writers to publicly denounce the Academy. The Academy represented the aristocratic upper classes, unlike this group of young artists who were democrats and socialists. They yearned to capture the reality and often-times the sordidness of the working class. They searched to capture man's entire spirit in his natural habitat, be it on the streets of Paris or in the countryside.

Once more, Cezanne submitted works to the Salon, and once more he was rejected. This time he received scathing and insulting reviews from the critics. Zola wrote a defense in *Le Figaro*, claiming that there was, ". . . no reason why one should not paint pig's trotters as one paints melons and carrots." This referred to an early work Cezanne had submitted to the 1863 Salon of the Rejected. That spring Cezanne left Paris and spent several months working in the Aix countryside.

He spent much of his time doing vivid watercolors and defending himself as an artist to his omnipresent father. His style moved away from the short, choppy strokes towards a smoother sweeping brushstroke. He continued his search for realistic detail modulated with atmosphere and emotion. This same year, Cezanne and his fellow painters discovered Pere Tanguy, a paint seller. Tanguy appreciated Cezanne's works and gladly exchanged paints for paintings. By the turn of the century, Tanguy would own the finest collection of works by Cezanne.

The Salon of 1868, marked the dissolution of academic prejudice. Among those selected by the official Salon were Manet, Monet, Pissarro, Renoir and Bazille. Cezanne, again was rejected, but not without making a vast impression upon his fellow artists. Zola reviewed the exhibit for *L'Evenement Illustre*. In his review he wrote:

The classic landscape is dead, killed by life and truth. No one would say today that nature needs to be idealized, that skies and water are vulgar ... Our landscapists set out from dawn ... They go and sit anywhere, ... finding everywhere a living horizon, with a human interest ... Certain landscapists have created a nature in the taste of their day ... They have created a nature of convention ... Naturalists of talent on the contrary are personal interpreters; they tanslate truths in original languages; ... They are above all human and mix their humanity in the least tuft of foliage they paint.

Cezanne was not alone in the search for truth in nature. However, his search would not come to an end with Impressionism. Unlike Monet, Cezanne refused to ignore the object by blurring the atmosphere. He emphasized all figures, objects and things as solid geometric shapes. He fought to fully express the sensations of nature, without losing the clarity and richness of her organisation. Eventually, Cezanne found this synthesis in geometrics, but not without sacrificing his initial emotional reaction to Nature.

By 1869, Cezanne returned to Paris to find Zola struggling to support himself, financially and emotionally. Zola's works scandalized Paris and he found journalistic work less and less rewarding. As the new year wore on, great changes occurred for both men. Zola began work on a new novel and Cezanne began his courtship with his future wife, Hortense Fiquet. Although he was still tormented by his fear of women, Cezanne found in Hortense a mother-like and unthreatening woman. She was warm, easy-going, and apparently without any pretense. Cezanne was slowly released from the everpresent anxiety of women. His works began to show a new confidence which fully emerged in the 1870's.

In addition to being influenced by Pissarro, Cezanne was inspired by Manet. This can be seen in "La Pendule de Marbre", 1869-1870. Although it is far more subdued than his previous works, it still evokes an unsettling feeling. The contrasts between the white tablecloth and the dark folds and background, the choice of objects and the painstakingly precise strokes of the brush, create a dynamic, yet highly composed painting. The lines and directional slashes which will become a key in his later works, are introduced in "La Pendule de Marbre". The red horizontal slash in the shell contrasted against the vertical dark slash of the tablecloth, highlighted by the solidity of form all unify into an exquisitely tense composition.

The Franco-Prussian war broke out in 1870 and marked the fall of the Empire. Cezanne had left Paris with Hortense and returned to Southern

France. Napoleon's reign had ended and on September 5, France became a Republic. During the ensuing months Cezanne hid out in l'Estaque spending his days painting landscapes. However, his fears of being drafted into the army and of the war itself, gave rise to dark and brooding colors. The canvases from this period are overwhelming sad and lonely. The views of l'Estaque are filled with blacks, deep reds and are seething with turmoil. The brushstrokes are violent and sharp, creating a dramatic, swirling space.

In the period following the first year at l'Estaque, Cezanne continued to explore a variety of themes and techniques. In a comparison between the "Temptation of Saint Anthony" and "Une Moderne Olympia" we see two very different versions of classical themes. "The Temptation" theme for Cezanne was an exploration into his own fear and anxiety about women. However, the depiction shows a monk, dedicated to a life of celibacy and intellectual pursuit, drawn out of his loneliness by a woman. Coincidentally, Cezanne had just become involved with Hortense and he too, was being seduced by a woman. Compared to "Une Moderne Olympia", painted several years later, we find a flippant parody of Manet's "Olympia". The difference lies in Cezanne's newly found confidence. The reclining woman is basking in sensuality, uninhibited by the artist's own insecurities. Cezanne no longer found women debilitating, rather he had come to appreciate their warmth and sensuality.

In late 1871, Cezanne returned to Paris and renewed his artistic search in the company of old friends. Within a short time, Hortense bore him a son, Paul. Their domestic life in Paris became unbearable in a tiny apartment, leaving little space for Cezanne to paint. Thus, Cezanne, Hortense and Paul moved to Pontoise, the village where Pissarro was living. This marked the beginning of Cezanne's major development as an artist. Over the next three years, under the watchful eye of Pissarro and the peacefulness of Pontoise, Cezanne's struggles came to fruition.

Pissarro and Cezanne spent every day painting out-of-doors, Cezanne constantly watching and listening to Pissarro. Together they explored the impressionist's color values and effects of light. Cezanne attempted to translate his passionate nature into controlled, small and precise brushstrokes. Pissarro taught him to see and to think before he painted. Cezanne later recalled this relationship as one of father and son.

Another influence upon Cezanne's life during this period in Pontoise was Dr. Paul Gachet, an eccentric but exceedingly kind man. Gachet had always been drawn to artists in Paris and continued to do so when he moved to Auvers. Soon

Cezanne found a second person with whom he could be totally at ease. In fact, the Cezanne family soon rented a home in Auvers to be closer to Gachet.

The effect of Pissarro can be seen in Cezanne's "View of Auvers" and "Le Cour de Perme a Auvers". The colors have lightened dramatically and the strokes are short and delicate. The effect of light as it bounces off one roof onto the next is the direct result of Pissarro's teaching Cezanne to 'see'. The sense of depth is created by overlapping objects and the extremely subtle gradation of color. We no longer feel the overbearing melancholy and emotional crisis found in the earlier works at l'Estaque. There is a new and exhilarating freedom of spirit which was rarely present in the past.

In "La Maison du pendu", we also see a change in Cezanne's style. The control over his impetuousness is evident in the small strokes and disciplined use of color. Once again he has layered the paint to attain a sense of depth. Cezanne explained this by stating, "Because I can't render my sensation at a blow (du premier coup). So I lay on color, I keep laying it on as best I can. But when I begin, I seek always to paint sweepingly . . ." Thus, in "La Maison du pendu" we no longer see the black outlines of objects that isolate each area, yet there is still a sense of blocky patches, solidly immoveable.

It was also during this period that Cezanne grasped the problem of organizing his canvas with masses and volumes in depth. Under the influence of Pissarro, his works became less bulky, yet the objects remained solid, maintaining their integrity through a controlled gradation of color tonalities. The effect of Impressionism was felt by Cezanne through Pissarro. Its liberation of form and color opened the door for Cezanne's ultimate goal of harmonizing all the elements of nature with man.

In the spring of 1874, the majority of Impressionists, including Renoir, Monet, Degas, Sisley, Pissarro and Cezanne, organized an exhibit to counter the official Salon. The reaction to the exhibition was similar to that of the Salon of the Rejected. The established critics ridiculed the works as being absurd and ridiculous. One critic found Cezanne's "Une Moderne Olympia" to be, ". . . material for laughter . . . M. Cezanne can only be a bit of a madman, afflicted while painting with 'delirium tremens'. . . The critic continued by writing that Cezanne's landscapes, ("Etude a Auvers" and "La Maison du pendu"), ". . . are more than we can swallow".

However, all was not lost for Cezanne. He sold "La Maison du pendu" to Comte Doria and for the first time, the motley group attained public recognition as the 'Impressionists'. In 1875,

Renoir introduced Cezanne to Victor Choquet, a quiet, but arduous art collector. They soon became close friends through their mutual love of Delacroix. Choquet bought one of Cezanne's early Bathers. Although Cezanne's paintings were rejected by the official Salon in 1875 and 1876, he did not exhibit with the rest of the Impressionists at the Galleries Durand-Ruel in 1876. Instead, he returned to l'Estaque and began two sea views for Victor Choquet. In a letter to Pissarro, Cezanne wrote of his new perception of color-gradation. As he stated, "The sun is so frightening here that it seems to me as if objects were silhouetted not only on black and white but in blue, red, brown and violet. I may be mistaken but this seems to me the antipodes of modelling. "Cezanne's future guidelines of color modulation were crystallized that summer in the South. The delicate balance of color is fully evident in "Paysage de Provence". In this watercolor, Cezanne has used extremely light brushstrokes to gently ease from one area of color to the next. The effect of sun light can be seen darting from tree to tree and background to foreground. The overall feeling is one of airy freshness held within a tightly balanced composition.

Upon his return to Paris, Cezanne found his good friend Zola once more in the throes of literary scandal. Like the works of the Impressionists, Zola's novels outraged the public and the critics.

This reinforced Cezanne's growing disgust for the bourgeoisie and solidified his militancy as a socialist.

The first official Impressionist Exhibition was held in 1877. Cezanne exhibited sixteen works, including a portrait of Choquet, still lifes, landscapes and one of his Bathers. In the "Portrait of Victor Choquet" we sense the same lightness and freedom found in the new landscapes. There is also a hint of romanticism in the pensive expression in Choquet's eyes. Perhaps this is the way that Choquet viewed himself. Cezanne has captured the atmoshere of Choquet, yet without ignoring his actual physical presense.

The Impressionist Exhibition was received with generally more tolerance than it had been in the past. However, Cezanne's works still provoked intense hostility. One critic described him as, "A real intransigent, hotheaded and fantastical." This controversy was heated by G. Riviere's review in *L'Impressioniste,* the journal published by the exhibition. Riviere unconditionally praised Cezanne in the following excerpt:

> M. Cezanne is a painter and a great painter . . .
> His beautiful still lifes, so exact in tonal relationships, have a solemn quality of truth . . .
> His canvases have the calm, the heroic serenity of ancient paintings and terracottas, and the ignoramuses who laugh before the 'Baigneuses', for

example, have on me the effect of barbarians criticizing the Parthenon.

Unfortunately, G. Riviere was only one of a handful of loyal supporters. In the face of disasterous criticism Cezanne never again exhibited with the Impressionists.

That summer Zola went South while Cezanne remained in Paris. Zola had finally achieved acceptance and success with his novel, *L'Assomoir,* and was able to afford a summer at L'Estaque. Cezanne stayed with Pissarro in Auvers with trips into Paris. During one of these sojourns, Cezanne met a young stockbroker who purchased several canvases. The young banker's name was Gauguin. Many new artists were arriving in Paris and formed a circle around Pere Tanguy's paint shop. Cezanne was amongst those whose works Tanguy kept alive and on exhibit in the store.

In the early spring of 1878, Cezanne returned to Southern France, leaving Hortense at Marseilles and himself commuting between Aix and l'Estaque. However, difficulties soon arose between Cezanne and his father, who threatened to cut-off his monthly allowance. It was to Zola that Cezanne turned. Throughout the year of 1878, Zola helped to support the Cezanne family.

During this year of financial struggle, Cezanne worked towards the unification of color with his personal vision. He also began to explore the use of color in receding planes to achieve harmony between depth and tone. Cezanne ultimately discovered that through the interaction of colored planes he could realize a dynamic sense of depth which went beyond the static concept of immobile objects in space. Each element in the painting was held in a momentary harmony, checked and balanced by the continuous color scheme of planes.

This new technique can be seen in the "Chateau de Medan". The vertical, horizontal and diagonal brushstrokes create a tension between the various planes. There is a sense of vibrant motion within the parts, yet the whole is harmonious. We experience a sense of receding depth, simultaneously, with an unexpected sense of direct contact. It is through an understanding of these paradoxes that it is possible to comprehend Cezanne's struggle to harmonize two opposing forces.

In 1880, Cezanne returned to Paris to discover his good friend Zola in the throes of unprecedented success, following the publication of *Nana*. However, Cezanne's life seemed to be going in the opposite direction. He saw very few people and he refused to paint from live models. All the insecurities and problems which had plagued Cezanne as a young man had returned. He insisted on maintaining his Bohemian style of dress which served to alienate Zola's newly formed circle of friends. Cezanne became increasingly ill-at-ease with strangers and rapidly became a recluse. The following three years were marked by more rejections from the Salon, although the works of Renoir and Monet were accepted. This was accompanied by the critic's claim that Cezanne was one of those Impressionists who would never fulfill his potential.

During this period, Cezanne's style vascillated from parallel brushstrokes and interacting planes to sharply frenetic, comma-like strokes. He continued to explore the color-plane method in an effort to express greater depth and solidity without added massiveness. However, Cezanne completed very few works, leaving behind numerous drawings, sketches and half-finished canvases. Of the works that were completed, "La Maison du jas de Bouffan", "Marroniers du jas de Bouffan" and "La Montaigne au Grand Pin" were outstanding examples of landscapes. The works are all carefully constructed, minutely thought out and perhaps even a bit too intellectual and dry. The emphasis on the linear elements, as in the trees in "Marroniers", is a departure from Cezanne's previous explorations into color-plane technique. Yet, a superb balance is achieved by contrasting broad horizontal bands of color.

Returning to the context of built up color-planes, Cezanne explored the effect of a different brushstroke in "Vue de Gardanne". He used small, comma-like strokes to express constant motion of the trees. The sense of depth is achieved by over-lapping color-planes, forcing the eye to be drawn into the background. Although there is a distinct contrast between the red of the roof tops and the green of the trees, the total effect remains tranquil.

Throughout the 1880's, Cezanne continued to be drawn to the sea coast at l'Estaque. He applied Impressionist technique in conjunction with his own acute sense of color in, "Le Golfe de Marseille, vu de l'Estaque". The vivid reds and rich blues are placed within Cezanne's own panoramic vision. An even earlier work, "La Montaigne Marseilleveyre et l'ile Marie", clearly indicates Cezanne's experimentation with precise vertical and horizontal brushstrokes to achieve planar depth.

It was during these years of frustration, that Cezanne executed some of his finest still lifes. In "Still Life a la Commode", Cezanne has strongly contrasted the stark whiteness of the tablecloth against the dark, ambiguous background. The solidity of the cloth and fruit is emphasized by the dark, almost black outlines. This weighty treatment differs greatly from the sublety found in "La Vase Bleu". The entire painting is a masterful play of tonal gradation. The changing tone of blue is delicately varied throughout the painting. The composition is extremely formal, yet the individual elements are relaxed, almost whimsical. We are brought very close to the work, but the background recedes into vertical and diagonal shades of blue. "La Vase Bleu", painted by Cezanne during an extremely difficult time in his life, is a virtual gem of subtlety.

Another theme which Cezanne continued to explore was the bathers series. In the 1880's, one in particular stands out, his single male bather, "Le Baigneuse". In this painting we are confronted by an isolation from 'humanness'. There are none of the usual nymphs celebrating nature and the human body. Rather, we find a solitary figure, like a statue placed in a landscape. The body and limbs virtually echo the landscape in its color, starkness and spartan detail. The angles of the arms are reinforced by the mountain's slope in the background. The dark outlines of the figure serve to restrain its movement. Yet, there is a dynamism in the torso which fractures the overall meditative quality of the painting.

In addition to the many aesthetic problems Cezanne wrestled with, his personal problems intensified. He developed a phobia about physical contact, which put an end to all sexual relations with Hortense. This must have further shattered his already shaken confidence. On April 4, 1886,

Cezanne wrote Zola a letter acknowledging receipt of his new novel, *L'Oevre*. It was essentially a farewell note, for the main character, Claude, was based on a tragic interpretation of Cezanne's life. Zola described Claude/Cezanne as an impotent genius and a failure who ultimately committed suicide. This so distressed Cezanne, that he ended their life-long friendship.

Several weeks later, Cezanne married Hortense after years of coercion from his parents. This did not improve their relationship, rather it marked an official separation; Hortense moved to Paris with their son, Cezanne remained in Aix with his mother. That October, Cezanne's father died, leaving in his will a small fortune to Cezanne. Thus freed from financial burdens, Cezanne was also freed from the everpresent love/hate obsession with his father. The effect was wildly liberating, driving Cezanne into a frenzied push forward.

Following the death of his father, Cezanne's works seem to take on an objective coolness. "Self Portrait at Easel", is perhaps the best example of this remoteness. Meyer Schapiro has described the painting as, "one of the most impersonal self-portraits we know . . ." The formal composition of the work is rigid and monumental. The painter does not face the observer, but the canvas, whose color is virtually the same as the skin-tone. It is as if Cezanne felt no sense of self while painting. The rectangular shapes of the palette and canvas are repeated throughout the body of the artist. The solid rectangles sharply overlap each other, foreshadowing the future techniques of the Cubists. However, within the rigidity, Cezanne again employed delicate tonal gradations on the palette and in the background. This created a sense of inner freedom despite the overall severity of the composition.

In 1888, Cezanne returned to Paris for two years. At the request of Victor Choquet, Cezanne painted a mardi gras scene of Pierrot with a harlequin. Cezanne used his son as the model for the harlequin. Unlike many other depictions of this scene, Cezanne's "Mardi Gras" is very formal and unexpressive. However, the delicacy of form and the precision of the brushstrokes offset the alienation of feeling. Cezanne has frozen his momentary glance into the world of "Mardi Gras".

During his stay in Paris, Cezanne divided his time between the Louvre and Tanguy's store. It was at Tanguy's shop that Cezanne met Vincent Van Gogh, a budding, young artist. Ironically, after viewing Van Gogh's work, Cezanne proclaimed, "Truly you paint like a madman". Unfortunately, it was Cezanne who was closer to the 'madman'. His temperament became more erratic and his physical health began to deteriorate from diabetes. Upon his return to Aix, he fell more and more under the control of his mother and sought even greater isolation from people.

His works during this period continued to show objectivity and intellectual clarity. However, his "Portrait of Madame Cezanne in the Conservatory" is an exception. In it we see an unusual tenderness and expressiveness. The far away, dream-like state of Madame Cezanne is most unusual. The repetition of the tilt of her head in the angle of the tree and the potted plant seems to emphasize her oneness with the environment. Perhaps it was Cezanne's attempt to display all of his hidden emotions for his wife.

While at Aix, Cezanne became a devout churchgoer. He hoped to find a crutch on which he could burden all of his inner anxieties. Apparently, Cezanne felt more secure for he returned to using live models and he also resumed painting portraits. One of the first themes Cezanne pursued with live models was the card players. Throughout the 1890's Cezanne returned to this motif. In each new work Cezanne deliberately avoided expressing the emotions of the game, i.e., competitiveness, excitement or greed. Rather he captured a moment of intense concentration, a brief moment when all of the players consider their hands and hold internal dialogues. The players are oblivious to each other and all possible spectators. Cezanne chose this exceedingly personal moment, reflecting his own subjective perceptions. He applied his subjective vision to events and objects found in nature and the real world.

Another figure study which revealed Cezanne's search for monumentality within subjective expression is "Le Garcon au gilet rouge". The young boy is caught in an overwhelmingly depressed reverie. His shoulders are limp, his eyes and vague countenance are downcast. With the exception of the red vest, the colors are cool and sad. However, within the forms are active and passionate brushstrokes, which vibrate against the massive forms.

Cezanne continued this exploration into subjective expression with still-lifes. In 1895, he painted "L'Amour en Platre," in which we find a cast of Puget's cupid and in the upper right corner, a study for The Flayed Man. Both are Baroque figures, in that they are curvilinear and highly animated subjects. However, only Cezanne would choose to place these two monumental and classic figures amidst onions and apples. This choice, said to the world that Cezanne, and only Cezanne could unite the heroic with the mundane, the spirit of passion with nature.

By the early 1890's, Paris had begun to take notice of Cezanne. This was stimulated by numerous articles on the works of Cezanne by George

Lecomte, Bernard, Zola and Gustave Geffroy. In 1894, Pere Tanguy died and a leading art dealer, Vollard, bought five Cezanne paintings from Tanguy's estate. At the same time, Geffroy's article was published, praising Cezanne as "the precursor of Gauguin and Van Gogh." In the spring of 1895, Cezanne asked Geffroy to pose for him. Although unfinished, the portrait of Gustave Geffroy, is one of Cezanne's finest works. Cezanne seated Geffroy at a desk in his library, surrounded by objects with which Geffroy is immediately identified. The figure is an immobile, solid mass, seated amongst the animated clutter of his daily life. The books are sharply angled on different shelves and the open books on the desk are virtually alive. The angularity is relieved by the small nude statue and the tulip in the vase on the left. We are confronted by an intense feeling for Geffroy, the man and his environment. Within all of the structure and composition, there remains the vibrant feeling for the spirit of Gustave Geffroy.

Cezanne was extremely productive in the mid-1890's. Vollard organized Cezanne's first one-man show, which to the surprise of all sold more works than ever before. In fact, several critics began to view his works with open minds and encouraging words. This newly found success uplifted the spirits and renewed Cezanne's confidence. His still-lifes took on a new vivacity of color. In "Pommes et Oranges", we see a celebration of reds and oranges. Cezanne had broken out of the table-as-frame motif by using the entire canvas as the frame. It is overflowing with vibrant drapery and multi-colored background. The contrast of white, with red and purple sing out in a truly orchestrated celebration of nature. "Pommes et Oranges" is Cezanne's most joyous 'un-still-life'.

The feeling of exaltation was carried into all of the landscapes during this period. In "Le Grand Pin" we are confronted by a magnificent portrait of a pine tree. Cezanne painted the tree as he would a man; a lone individual frought with pain and scars from the outside world. The strength and magnitude of the tree, against a background of blue-green is truly monumental. With small, deliberate brushstrokes, Cezanne created the eternal effect of the wind upon all the leaves, without distinguishing one single leaf from the entirety of nature.

The year of 1897 marked the beginning of artistic maturity for Cezanne. It also found two Cezanne paintings hanging in the Luxembourg Museum as part of the Caillebotte collection. Working out of his studio in Paris, Cezanne painted "La Jeune Italienne", using the same rich and complex color scheme found in "Pommes et Oranges", yet the overall effect is very different. The young woman is filled with great simplicity and nobility. The upper part of her body cuts a broad diagonal across the top half of the canvas which is balanced by the dark blue skirt and drapery. The table upon which she leans, is far from solid, rather it is richly decorated with a pattern that defies solidity. Again, Cezanne has remarkably created strong masses that are comprised of small, atom-like particles.

By the end of the century, Vollard had become Cezanne's dealer. With help from Cezanne's son, Vollard began to sell Cezanne's paintings. In the same year, Cezanne painted a portrait of Ambroise Vollard, which was finally completed after over one-hundred and fifty sittings. He had spent the last several years visiting Aix, Paris and Fontainbleu. In Aix, Cezanne had discovered a farmhouse whose view he grew to love almost as much as L'Estaque. He painted Chateau Noir numerous times over a period of ten years. In addition to this new landscape, Cezanne continued to explore the bathers, Mont Ste. Victoire, still-lifes and portraiture.

The remainder of Cezanne's life was spent in Aix, painting from models and in the open-air. In 1900, three works of Cezanne were hung at the Petit Palais, as part of the International Exhibition. Cezanne also exhibited three works with the Salon des Independents. Thus, Cezanne's reputation was spreading to those outside the realm of painters and critics. In 1901, Cezanne built a studio in Aix, with a view of the mountains. From 1902 until his death, Cezanne stayed at his studio and tried to rediscover the Provencal countryside.

By 1903, Cezanne's reputation had grown dramatically with the public, but privately he was continually plagued by doubts. At times, he felt he was approaching his artistic goals, yet there were days of deep frustration and depression. However, his art took on grand proportions, or as Meyer Schapiro described it as having "epic largeness".

In Cezanne's largest canvas, "Les Grandes Baigneuses", we readily see the "epic largeness". The women are no longer the erotic seducers found in "The Temptation of St. Anthony". They have transcended their humanity to become classically monumental. Their nobility is reinforced by the classic triangular composition, the base of which is formed by the bathers, and the two sides of the triangle is formed by the limbs of the trees. The women's bodies are no longer constrained in studio-model poses. They are frozen in an intense moment of thought, as if a camera had caught them unaware. It is precisely the spontaneity within the figures, illuminated by flesh-tones and sparkling blues, which creates a sense of vitality within a strong and formal composition.

The spontaneity of the "Baigneuses" is extended even further in the very last works by Cezanne. In "Mont Ste. Victoire", we can see a total release from constraint. The colors leap off the canvas in an ecstatic celebration of nature. Mont Ste., Victoire dramatically soars to the sky which explodes around the peak. Cezanne had offered himself to Nature and finally, in return, received all of her dynamic creativity.

During the summer of 1906, Cezanne was confined to his studio in Aix. His sole companion was his gardner, Vallier. In one of his last works, Cezanne painted a magnificent portrait of Vallier. He returned to the common man, with all of his simplicity, integrity and strength. As in the portrait of Gustave Geffroy, we feel most intensely not the details of Vallier, but the very essence of the man. We learn of Vallier's tranquility and self-sufficiency amidst the lively brushstrokes and incandescent color. It is in this last work, that we feel Cezanne's search for nobility and strength within mankind come to an end.

In September, 1906, eight paintings by Cezanne were accepted by the Autumn Salon. The joy Cezanne felt over this final and long coming recognition would not be long lived. Several days after being caught in a rainstorm, Paul Cezanne died on October 22, 1906. Cezanne's life had been plagued with personal and professional failures. In the end, Paul Cezanne triumphed, forging the principles of Modern 20th Century Art.

LIST OF COLOR PLATES

THE PLATES

1
Self-Portrait
1861

2
The orgy
1864-1868

3
The orgy (detail)
1864-1868

5
Still life with a skull and a candlestick
1865-1867

A modern Olympia
1873

The temptation of St. Anthony
1867-1869

8
Cupid in plaster
1895

9
Paul Alexis reading a manuscript by Zola
1869-1870

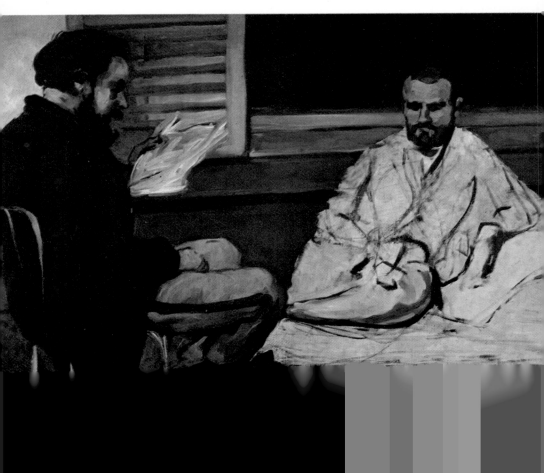

10
Man in a cotton cap
1867

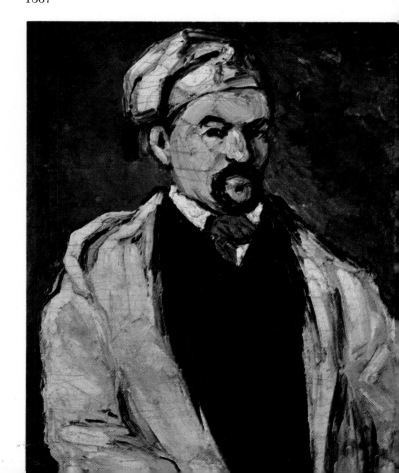

11
Still life with a tin teapot
1869-1870

12
The blue vase
1885-1887

13
Portrait of Gustave Geffroy
1895

14
Woman with a coffee pot
1890-1894

15
View of Gardanne (watercolor)
1886

16
Rocky landscape (watercolor)
1895

17
Portrait of Ambrose Vollard
1899

18
Portrait of Vallier
1906

19
Apples and oranges
1895-1900

20
Still life with a basket of apples
1894

21
Mount Marseilleveyre and the Ile Maire (watercolor)
1882-1885

22
Rocks beneath trees
1894-1898

The Gulf of Marseilles, view from L'Estaqu◄
1883-188；

24 Cezanne. Paysage au toit Rouge. Countryside with red roof.

26
Mount Sainte Victoire with a large pine tree
1885-1887

27
Poplars
1879-1882

28
The road and the pond
1879-1882

29
Nymphs at the seashore
1890-1894

30
Male bathers
1892-1894

32
Self-portrait
1880-1881

33
The house of Dr. Gachet at Anvers
1873

34
Courtyard of a farm at Anvers
1873

35
House and tree
1873

36
House of the hanged man
1873

Intersection of Remy Street at Anvers
1876

The house at "Jas de Bouffan"
1885-1887

39
Chestnut trees at "Jas de Bouffan"
1885-1887

40
House behind trees
1885-1887

41
Trees and houses
1885-1887

42
Rocks and branches at Bibemus
1900-1904

43
View of the black chateau
1894-1896

44
Landscape of Provence (watercolor)
1875-1878

46
A bouquet with china
1873-1875

47
A glass and apples
1879-1882

48
Portrait of Louis Guillaume
1888

49
Italian girl leaning on her elbow
1896

50
Pot of flowers with pears
1888-1890

51
Pot of geraniums with fruits
1890-1894

53
The card players
1890-1892

54
House on the Marne
1888-1890

55
The Maincy Bridge
1882-1885

56
Still life with onions
1895-1900

57
Still life with a job of milk
1888-1890

58
Boy with a red vest
1894-1895

59
Boy with a red vest
1894-1895

60
Portrait of the dwarf, Emperaire
1866

61
Portrait of the dwarf, Emperaire (study in charcoal)
1868

62
Harlequin
1888-1890

63
Mardi-Gras
1888

65
Large female bathers
1898-1905

66
Still life with a commode
1883-1887

67
Still life with a soup pot
1880-1885

68
Madame Cezanne
1895

69
Self-portrait with palette
1885-1887

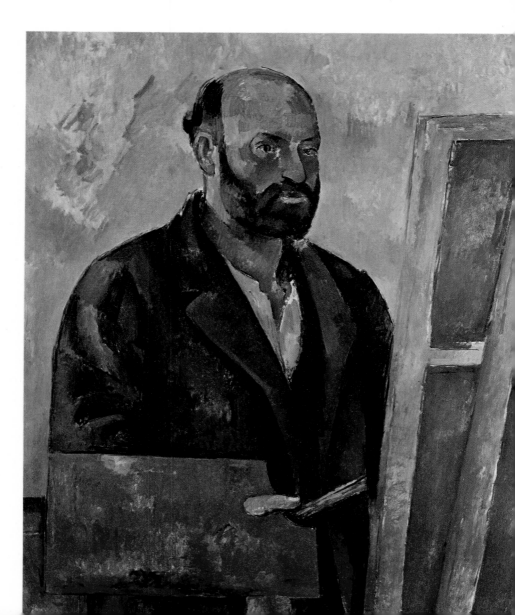

70
Mount Sainte Victoire and the black chateau
1895-1900

71
Road winding in front of Sainte Victoire
1895

72
Still life (watercolor)
1890-1894

73
Chair, bottle and apples (watercolor)
1906

74
Mount Sainte Victoire
1904-1906

75
The red rock
1904-1906